Along the Way

Charlotte Lit Press
Charlotte Center for Literary Arts, Inc.
PO Box 18607
Charlotte, NC 28218
charlottelit.org/press

Cover photo by Joe Spencer

ISBN: 978-1-960558-06-0

PROUD MEMBER

[clmp]

COMMUNITY OF LITERARY MAGAZINES & PRESSES
W W W . C L M P . O R G

Along the Way

Joe Spencer

Charlotte Center for Literary Arts, Inc.
Charlotte, North Carolina
charlottelit.org

To my partner, Gala Palmer, who encouraged my early, short, flirtatious verses to become the more fully developed poems in this collection.

Contents

Turning

a poem in haiku stanzas

Once, in a scrap heap,
I searched for my counterpart—
to make an object.

I was drawn to you
for your flowing grain, strength
and silent wisdom,

Your shape, yet unknown,
begging for a second chance
to be of service,

Your imperfections,
showing novel character
and tortuous growth.

Reshaping beauty—
I turned you into three cups
and we were all pleased.

Which was more transformed—
this recreated turner
or your flowing grain?

Epitaph for Innocence

You had been different—
above the barnyard chatter.
We felt without touching, knew
without knowing. Seeking solitude
with me in this world was your mistake.
I let you become caught up in the day's fate.

You were carried to the chopping block. I was given an axe.
Your life was about to end while mine, at age ten, was coming
of age. My weak grip around your neck held your head
against the chopping block. Yet, made eye contact. You
became a being—silent, brave, wise—accepting that our
time on earth together was about to end. You knew that
my pounding heart, shaking hand and sick stomach were
not in this, and forgave me. Caught between my cowardice
and your sympathy for my plight, I felt your softness, your
warmth, your understanding—that this would be our
last act together. Frozen in horror I allowed the axe to be
grabbed from my hand.

I lost your love, but gained another companion that day—
Guilt—and it has spoken to me every day since. Carved
into my clean slate—your execution was the epitaph for
my innocence.

Filed Away

"I'll look for your application in the file
and send you something," the young lady,
manager trainee, told the once proud man
now applying for the position of Walmart greeter.

"I would like to know if I have been passed over.
Is my application still under consideration?"

Back outside again, in never-never land,
      between vibrant and elderly,
      between useful and used up,
      between maladies,
      between naps,

He drifts,
      head bent, back stooped,
      full of contrition
      for some unknown sin,

Searching,
      for one last fulfilling thing.

The Last Thing Darkness Reveals

Ambushed, sucker punched, T-boned—
the recent "unpleasantness"
changed blue to gray
and everything else to black.

My songbird,
once singing and preening
and looking for the next new thing,
froze on its branch.

With time, the cloud lifted.
Sunbeams and sunsets,
rainbows and rim lit clouds
were a joy again.

The air smelled fresh,
there was a melody in the distance,
work had purpose,
and hope replaced defeat.

Then I recalled,
the last thing darkness reveals is
the light.

Romancing the Stream

First light unveils her,
shimmering in chilled darkness.
Swift currents guard an uncharted path
toward her hidden treasures.

Softly, I step, balance, step, wade, balance, stretch…
footrest to footrest…stout rock to silky bed to sunken log,
some polished and refined, some velvety,
some loose and capricious, I teeter
over slippery shapes like a baby learning to walk.

The sun has joined us now, revealing her power and beauty.
Crashing rapids play like a brawling brass band,
trying to pull me into their quarrel,
taking no notice of my frail baton.

Mystical forms and fissures threaten to topple me—
my heart races. Surely, a sharp tug on this sheer line
would do me in, the headlines reading
Angler in Prime of Life Drowned by Six Inch Brookey.

Like an unready lover
trepidation turns to pleasure
with her frigid, yet sensual caress.

For a time, we touch and talk,
my quiet thoughts, her subdued roar,
until she is not so threatening as before.

After lunch and rest I miss her touch,
her moist breath in my ear, her splendor…
and so…wanting to be closer…
I leave the waders ashore.

Gone Fishing

In my troubled youth
the 'gone fishing' approach to life
became a habit.

Fishing filled my need for escape.
Yet, catching fish was not what I wanted—
it was Nature's beauty
that hid a larger drama than mine.

Fishing was just the backdrop
for the black water and jagged undercuts
that hid the sinister shape
that snatched lives of

the small, the innocent, the careless—
a silt contrail the only evidence
of another life's passing.

Reunion

Again, we are drawn through soft, familiar mountains
    to the well-worn home place,
        its hearty greetings, warm smiles
           and once-a-year relatives.

Anxious children dance
    in anticipation
        of adventures
           with last year's playmates.

Conversation and laughter
    overflow the frail house
        like the tasty food
           crowding our handheld paper plates.

Favorite recipes and best stories are repeated
    as watchful mothers divide their attention
        between polite gossip, laughter
           and children's screams of joy.

Wooden decoys and our
    Would-be wooden men
        ring a resting field
           awaiting unsuspecting doves.

Grave philosophers
    gather under a tin-roofed porch,
        ponder deep problems, grasp for utopian ideals
           like pacifism and ending world hunger,

Their dreams
    interrupted by earthly reality
        as nearby small cannon fire and raining birdshot
           rattle their lofty sentiments and fragile shelter.

This Political Season

Our relationship distant,
      conversations guarded,
           again, this season
we step

from my sunken log
      to your slippery rock
           as our streams met.

Attention given
           to not falling
      into the chill,
into the shrill,

you went upstream,
      and I went down
           to wonder

would our streams
      ever bend again
           and allow another

chance meeting?

I Need a Better Group of Friends

My smartphone has turned me into a smartass.
It is so easy to critique Facebook blather
in lieu of listening, laughing,
and loving.

Edgy jokesters shout "look at me"
as they mug for the multitudes,
and cast about for a persona
other than, 'I'm lonely'.

Needy, desperate—
cartoon characters sharing what they had for lunch—
these Facebook 'Friends' hoping for a 'Like'
have rendered my curser motionless.

Where did that weekend with the family go?
The tweet drama monster ate it
and turned my dumb joke into WWIII
with Facebook multitudes I do not even know.

Come on, marinate those
half-baked wisecracks
before serving them
up to the world. Then,

Put them somewhere the sun never shines.

The Men's Club

For years there was something satisfying about this din, two
hundred of us, crowded close, the almost yelling conversational
tone.

Businessmen, we spoke varnished prose all week, but then
spoke our hearts about sports, back-in-the-day personal tales, all
inflated a little.

We were all friends for those few hours, Democrat and
Republican, Black and White, religious and non, it did not
matter (although those topics were notably absent).

We were bonded, we were tribal, back on the plain, sharing food
and heroic tales.

Yet, something was missing—

Something beyond our fervent brotherhood—
Something we were incomplete without—
Something that made us better—

Our most civilizing influence—

Women.

Growing Pains

Wednesday night church dinner and
joyful confusion at the hors d'oeuvres table—
so many choices—
       eyeing, feeling, smelling—
       a little girl's dilemma.

A white grape finally selected,
but only nibbled until—
finally, mercifully,
to everyone's relief
       it was swallowed—whole.

Nearing wit's end,
a mother's correction—
the world of the serious
intruding the world of the sensuous.

Such are the trials of a little girl,
       to be pure—
       to be sure—
       to before—
       to becoming—

       a lady,

skinned knees and all.

Ode to the Librarian

Wealthy and wise,
the patron,
intent upon his Times,
sees the World in print, but not this one:

Riveted to their computers,
the jobless,
hoping to get back in the loop or,
just back to loved ones.

Bags filled,
like squirrels planning for winter,
readers taking books to their dens
to escape tonight's boredom.

Infants shrieking
their joy of being alive,
their protest against
quietness.

While she floats behind desks,
between stacks,
among patrons,
taking whispered cues,

Without pretense,
anxious to please,
the master of all she surveys—
the librarian.

World Traveler from an Appalachian Holler

Born 7.4.1922 and raised in an Appalachian holler
in a cabin with outdoor plumbing, water piped from a stream,
now, a seatmate in business class, she had traveled the world.
Unknown in that moment, she was to tour London with me.

The next morning, caught in a light, freezing rain
I suggested a shortcut across London's Regent's Park.
Blind to the distance and her eighty-eight years,
arm-in-arm, we struck out.

Later, reliving our adventure,
she told friends I had 'drug her all over London,'
exaggerating in her humorous way
our miserable trek—and my mistake.

I knew she forgave me because the next day
we did it all over again, albeit in a different direction.
Such was her optimism,
coming from poverty, but rich in spirit.

How she became my best friend and toured London with me
is a long story that I do not even understand
(and I knew her for ten years).
Such was the spirit of this indomitable woman.

Her name was Mildred Lewis.
She died in her sleep on 7.5.21,
one day after her ninety-ninth birthday.

Alien Rap

Are there aliens
on a search
for more hospitable environs
like our blue and white pearl

that is the right distance from its star,
that rotates and wobbles
to produce abundant life
and its attendant strife,

that's adrift,
in uncertainty,
and mediocrity?

Since we're consumed by hate
they decide to just wait
because few heed the warning—
it's about to be too late.

We've forgotten our better days
when biology flourished
in the murky, earthly beginnings
we're ruining.

What drought and rising seas don't end,
they will easily rend
and master as the spoils
of our self-inflicted disaster.

'Hellucination'

"You will need to sit for 15 minutes before you leave,"
the sweet nurse instructed.

"Sure," I said,
before I froze, then dozed, lest anyone suppose
I was having a reaction.

As silence fell, there came the flu-like swell
that typically signaled
impending hell.

Then was the sound of a distant bugle
followed by the hoof-beats of the calvary charge
into the sinister creatures that surrounded me.

Sounds of slashing steel
and anguished screams
filled my ears.

Bodies and body parts
flew out of the skirmish
covering the once pristine landscape.

Then, as quickly as they came, they rode off
leaving only the dead and dying
to mark the battle.

Once again, the regiment
from Fort Immune
had saved me.

Release Me

Muse,

Please release me,
     from your whisper,

That draws me,
     from safety and shore,
     toward bottom, deeper,
     toward knowing.

Help me find,

Words,
     with syllables
     that fill the cadence,

Words,
     that give image
     its shape,

Words,
     that milk meaning
     from the moment.

Words,
     that get
     "Aha"—

Obviously,
     tonight's drug of choice.

An Engineer's Guide to Writing Poetry

Faded images begin life as a wordy essay,
edited for repetition, then shallowness
(which eliminates almost everything).

Ideas burst from hiding like flushed quail
desperate to escape the hunter's birdshot
(and the poet's ear).

Like beauty pageant entries—
ideas parade across the stage,
vying for the judge's attention.

And try to follow the rules of Poetland:
"Adjectives and adverbs will be rounded up, tried and executed.
Clichés will be shot on sight."

Perfection stops shadowboxing with Good
until finally, in time,
they come out of hiding—

Meaning, Meter and Rhyme.

Don't Make Mother Angry

We've mucked around with her long enough
and she ain't gonna take it no more.
Her climate, her soil, her oceans—
we robbed in the name of the almighty dollar.

The same Almighty
that gave us supersized—
that made us all
fat, dumb and happy.

Harnessed to debt
we could not afford,
we fed bankers
while our souls starved.

Her patience with us finally run out,
like water, she sent Little Covid to find a crack
to widen and make a flood.

She sent Little Covid to do a little culling.

It

For once It has me ready, on time.

I rarely stop It, but today I did.

Don't you want to know what It is?

It is something we all do,

but have stopped, or so we say,

but keep doing anyway.

It persists. It wastes us.

We all fall prey to—

It.

Don't you want to know what It is?

Sorry, you will have to wait

until I get around to—It,

this wolf that stole

my masterpiece

and much of

my life.

Adventures in Hitchhiking

With a weekend leave, little money, and my reliable thumb,
hitching a ride from downtown Tucson seemed a good idea.

The driver's hippie girlfriend slid over to let me ride shotgun.
A few minutes later I caught him eyeing my gold college ring,
which, if pawned, would help their dire financial condition.

Our front seat small talk turned to uncomfortable silence.
The guy in the back seat lost interest in his girlfriend
as his glazed-over eyes averted mine, nervously.

I wondered how to exit a moving car without dying.
At a welcomed red light about to turn green,
I smiled, made my exit stage right and said,

"Thanks for the ride" while, from behind,
An urgent honk hustled them along.

I have always benefited from
the kindness of strangers
like the one behind,

playing his horn for
this would-be
tragic opera.

How I Came by My Name

Originally, in Scotland and England,
people's names stood for their occupations.
Spencers were stewards, butlers, administrators.
Today, they are Eastern North Carolina farmers and carpenters.

My grandfather was a railroad engineer.
The largest metal toolbox anyone ever carried—
his contained outsized tools that kept the locomotives running.
In comparison, today's auto mechanics' wrenches are toys.

There are twenty gravestones of Spencers going back to the 1850s
in the old Pineville, North Carolina graveyard—
descendants of earlier arrivals to the New World from England
that landed in Wilmington, probably indentured servants.

Recalling Dad's brother, Tom, at the dinner table,
with his overpowering brogue
still heard in parts of eastern North Carolina reminds me—
no one ever won an argument with him.

Tom carved out a one-hundred-and-fifty-acre farm adjacent
to the Great Dismal Swamp, raised truck crops and tobacco.
Like his father and my dad, he had a lifelong problem
with alcohol that afflicted everyone and killed him.

The gravestones indicate the Spencers were hardy,
especially the women.
The story is, my grandfather 'rose from the dead' twice,
but it's more plausible he was just passed out.

Generations of alcoholism and abuse
have ended with me.

So has the lineage.

The Farmer Heard

The farmer heard
the John Deere call his name,
begging to be of service one last time.

Once strong, ready to spring to life,
now, only a proud, old infantryman,
standing at attention, awaiting orders.

Its battle with time near the end,
cloaked in orange, humbled,
it leaned against the wind.

Smaller now than in my youth,
without its once deep roar
it could only watch

as the forest plotted its advance
to reclaim the untilled acres,
while the wind whispered,

"A way of life is passing on."

Last Dance

The goddess Muse keeps irregular hours,
    gliding through my darkness,
        trailing fine hair and exotic flowers.

Thrilled by chance meeting
    and our search
        that wants completing,

With dreams unfolding,
    we spin
        toward deeper knowing,

Until the late-night chime
    disturbs our quest,
        for meaning, meter and rhyme.

Collateral Damage

Arguments are not lone events,
but ignite related, combustible things.

Will this small fire spread until
all that is tender is consumed,
before our better angels arrive,
before permanent harm is done?

We justify our fighting
as nature's way of
making room for the new.

Will our afflicted children,
caught in the inferno,
be among the ruins
of our madness?

Rocky Horror

Born of Mother Earth,
pristine granite became
today's majestic remnant—

the Rockies.

Other proud stones,
nourished by Wind and Rain
became tufted hills—

the Appalachians.

Both, on a slow march
to their final resting place,
along with you and me,

to become—

sand and muck.

Blessings

My childhood home became a branch bank
before being bought by the Church of God
who introduced me to Vacation Bible School.
Halleluiah!

Delivering the afternoon paper in the August heat
gave me a deep thirst—an obsession that continues to this day—
I cannot turn down an A&W Root Beer.
Thank you, Jesus!

Fishing a neighborhood pond gave me an appreciation
of Mother Nature, reflection,
and the world lying below the surface of everything.
Praise the Lord!

Acknowledgements

I wish to acknowledge my poetry cohort at Charlotte Lit, especially Dannye Romaine Powell, whose encouragement has been consistently helpful. I continue to be inspired by such poets as Collins, Frost, Sandburg and lesser known poets who have one thing in common: the ability to reignite the sense of wonder I've always had about the miracle of life.

Today, when I feel awestruck it is often a poem that did it.

About the Author

Joe Spencer is a native of Charlotte, North Carolina, a graduate of North Carolina State University, and a retired professional engineer. In addition to reading, volunteering, playing tennis, and sailing, he enjoys writing essays and poetry, some of which has been compiled into this first chapbook.

Printed in the USA
CPSIA information can be obtained
at www.ICGtesting.com
JSHW080818080224
56754JS00005B/188